Something's Amiss in My Uterus

Something's Amiss in My Uterus

Written By Hilary Hodes
Illustrated By Scott Hodes

SOMETHING'S AMISS IN MY UTERUS
Copyright © 2002 by U.S. Copyright Office

All rights reserved. No reproductions or portions may be reproduced in any form whatsoever without written permission.

Dedicated to Dillon Grant. . .you are our pride and joy; today, tomorrow, and always. Without you, this book would not be possible. Snugs, thanks to you, life is soooooooooooooo good!
I love you.

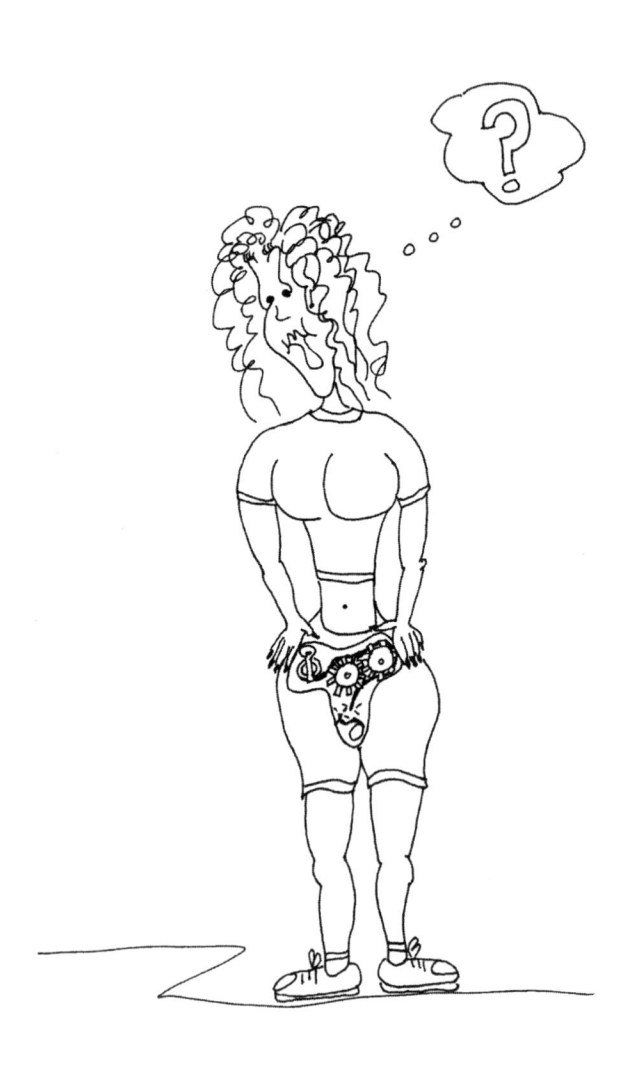

Something's Amiss in My Uterus

Something feels strange
Wonder what could it be,
Something is brewing
It's stewing inside me.

Yes, something is odd
And most surely amiss,
This something is stirring
In my own uterus.

Not sure what it is
But I have a clue,
That in just nine months,
I'll have loads to do.

Although I'm not certain
I believe it is so,
There are things in this world
That a woman does know.

For I am quite certain
That something's amiss,
Something is growing
In my uterus.

The Test for Which You Can't Study

Off to the drugstore
Away I must go,
Because 4-1-1
Has not this info.

I turn to the pharmacist,
"Which test should I take?"
He says it doesn't matter
Not one is a fake.

I take the closest test
Right off of the shelf,
And then calmly start
To talk to myself.

Today is the day
Yes, soon I will learn,
If my egg encountered
An industrious sperm.

Then into the car
Off to my abode,
I enter the house
Run to the commode.

Initially, the test
Is not easy to take,
I pee on the wrong side
And that's a mistake.

For a few hours,
I must sit and wait,
Until another stream comes
And I urinate.

Onto the stick
Here comes the flow,
Holy *!@#!%
And away we go!

The minutes feel like hours
As I long to see,
If a new limb will be added
To my family tree.

A positive test
A second red line,
No wonder I haven't
Been feeling so fine.

Let me be sure
I'll take one more try,
Yep... positive...
Is it a girl or a guy?

ME

Attention, world,
It's all about me,
And my new condition
It's called "pregnancy."

Every symptom I have
Is undoubtedly new,
And everything I feel
Is much different, too.

So sit up straight
Do try to follow,
I have much to tell,
My words you must swallow.

The fruits of my labor
And all of my work,
I am certain that I
Won't drive you berserk,

When I talk about me
And the baby all day,
Let's now pay attention
To the words that I say.

It's oh so obvious
Is it not easy to view,
Growing a fetus
Is not simple to do.

So don't stray from form
Concentrate on me,
My life is important,
I know you agree.

Excuse me but what
Did you say over there,
There is something you said
That I did overhear.

Now that can't be possible
How could it be true,
Could someone else be having
A baby that's due?

Mr. Couch is No Slouch

I look at the clock
It says almost five,
Why is it I barely
Am feeling alive?

I'm so very sleepy
I can hardly move,
It seems that I can't
Get into a groove.

I feel mighty weak
I'm extremely tired,
Look at my freshness date
The ink reads "expired."

My eyelids are heavy
They feel like a brick,
If I don't get to the couch
I'm gonna' be sick.

Behold there he is
My friend, Mr. Couch,
Call him anything
Except for a slouch.

He extends out his arms
And embraces me,
This is exactly
Where I want to be.

I sprawl across him
And there as I lay,
My body immediately
Starts to drift away.

Oh Mr. Couch
If every man were like you,
Every woman would be rested
And deliriously happy, too.

Will It...?

Will it be a she
Will it be a he,
Will it look like daddy,
Will it look like me?

Will it be a boy
Will it be a girl,
Will its hair be straight or
Will it have a curl?

Will it be feisty
Will it be calm,
Will it have my hands
When I gaze at its palm?

Will it be short
Will it be tall,
Will it be big
Will it be small?

Will its hair be blond
Will its locks be brown,
Will it smile a lot
Will it wear a frown?

Will its skin be dark
Or will it be fair,
Will its nose be pointed
Or shaped like a pear?

Will its eyes be hazel
Or will they be blue,
Will it look like me
Will it look like you?

I could ask the "Will it" questions
Day after day,
But still I will hope
And continue to pray,

That when baby arrives,
He or she will have good health,
For this would be worth more
Than all a queen's wealth.

Pregnancy Food Pyramid

Bagels, bread,
And mashed potatoes,
Hot dogs, hamburgers,
And tomatoes.

Doritos, salsa,
All kinds of chips,
Ice cream, milk shakes,
And tasty sips.

Reeses, Hershey's, and
Loads of Snickers,
The junk that you eat,
I eat quicker.

Pizza loaded
With gooey cheese,
Creamy sauces
Covering peas.

Cookies filled
With chocolate chips,
Sour cream
And fattening dips.

Bacon, toast,
Two or three eggs,
Big, fried, fattening
Chicken legs.

Candy, french fries,
Chocolate cake,
Why anything
That I can bake.

Pecans, walnuts,
And cashews,
Any nut
That I can choose.

Of course I'm watching
What it is that I eat,
My caloric intake
Has not missed a beat.

Off to the fridge,
Alas, I must go,
Solely to ensure
My baby does grow.

SUPER MOCHA FUDGE
Pizza
Chips
CAKE
ICE CREAM
Chocolate
Chip
CAK
ICE C
CHOCOL
BBQ CHIPPOS
JACK'S PIZZA

Porcelain Party

Hello, Mr. Toilet,
And how do you do,
I came by to deliver
Something special for you.

I am sorry to say
It's that same gift again,
That splatters so rudely
Across your porcelain.

Please don't be angry
Pinkish-brown suits your finish,
And in a few weeks
My nausea will diminish.

You're always there for me
With mouth open wide,
Thanks for letting go
Of your porcelain pride.

We've grown so close
You are so dear to me,
But how is it some
Only come here to pee?

Extra, Extra Read All About It... Everyone's Got an Opinion and I Don't Want It

"Excuse me," he said,
And she said, too,
"I know precisely
What you need to do.

You need to do that
You need to do this,"
Your advice is bringing me
Why, oh so much bliss.

Everyone seems
To know what I need,
Especially when it comes
To raising my seed.

They know it all
Have even chosen a name,
Their unwanted wisdom
It just can't be contained.

Continually they dispense
This unsolicited advice,
Under the pretense
That they're being nice.

Yet these people are missing
A bit of info,
And there is one fact
That they need to know.

If they knew so much
Then it's certainly clear,
I'd ask if I wanted
Their opinion to hear.

Whoosh

Whoosh...Whoosh...
The start of a being,
My ears can hardly
Believe what they're hearing.

A twinkle of light
Representing each beat,
An existence is confirmed
Every time it repeats.

As it flickers fast
My heart, too, does race,
A smile extends
Across my whole face.

Two hearts have created
One fragile, small heart,
From love, a creation
Will now make its start.

I carefully listen
As each whoosh I hear,
And on down my cheek
I do shed a tear.

Tears of joy
Confirming today,
That soon a child
Will be heading my way.

Whoosh...Whoosh...
What a wonderful sound,
Something so precious
This day I have found.

Whoosh...Whoosh...
Thanks to you above,
For bringing a heartbeat
Symbolizing true love.

What's in a Name?

Jody, Missy,
Ben, Josh, Seth,
Herman, Annie,
Hilary, Beth,

Dillon, Irwin,
Nancy, Scott,
Marsha, Peter,
Lisa, Dot,

Rachel, Tracy,
Meagan, Jay,
Julie, Kathy,
Susan, Ray,

Michael, Stephen,
Mathew, Zach,
Jerry, Henry,
Harry, Jack,

Kenny, Mark,
Billy, Bradley,
Katie, Hansel,
Harold, Hadley,

David, Elizabeth,
Jennifer, Dan,
Michelle, Maggie,
Rosalyn, Stan,

Tommy, Wendy,
Thelma, Tad,
Phillip, George,
Theresa, Chad,

Jeffrey, Natalie,
Charles, Wanda,
Ashley, Tiffany,
Edward, Rhonda,

Gary, Chris,
Kiley, Sherri,
Marcey, Leroy,
Sissy, Carrie,

From so many
Names you'll choose,
And no matter
What you'll lose.

Some family member
Will hate your choice,
And you'll get to hear
Their whiny voice.

Lights...Camera...Adorable

I lift up my shirt
Exposing my belly,
The technician applies
Some transparent jelly.

A rolly device
Across me does move,
Her intensity manifests
She has something to prove.

Evidence is provided
It appears on the screen,
The most beautiful fetus
That I've ever seen.

It punches and kicks
And moves with such grace,
I already adore
Its not yet formed face.

Although the picture
Is not very clear,
Soon the technician
Has something to share.

The picture confirms
And does without fail,
The blob on the screen
Is certainly male.

The image is fuzzy
And a little bit bright,
Yet, I won't forget
This heaven-sent sight.

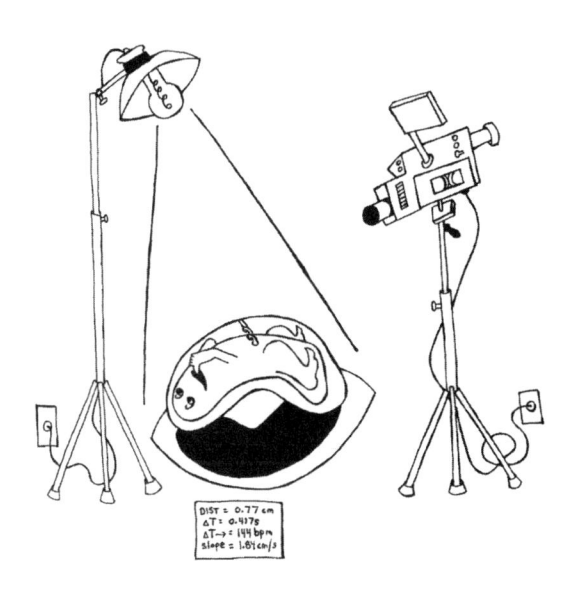

Kick Away

Whoa...what was that
A bubble burst inside me,
What on earth
Could it possibly be?

I look at my tummy
It's undulating out,
Something is moving
Of this there's no doubt.

Ouch, a hard one
To my rib, it's a kick,
When's the next strike
What spot will he pick?

Boom...pow...
There he goes again,
If he were a kickboxer,
He'd surely win.

Truth be told,
I should not really whine,
Every kick that I feel
Confirms that he's fine.

Ooof...wham...
Kick until you're content,
For I should be loving
Every kick that you've sent.

Kick away, kick away
Kick away, kick away,
Perhaps you will kick
Yourself out one day.

Mood Swings

I'm happy
No I'm sad,
I'm angry
No, I'm glad.

I want to go out
I want to stay in,
I want to do good
Wait, I want to sin.

I love the shade of black
It makes me look slight,
But lately I think
I prefer the color white.

Sometimes I feel hot
And later I'm cold,
I'm feeling quite shy
Yet now I feel bold.

Hurry up please
You're going too slow,
You're moving too fast
For me don't you know?

I'm hungry, I need
To consume food right now,
I can't eat a thing
For I'm as fat as a cow.

I'm feeling quite calm
No, I want to fight,
I need to turn left
Unless I turn right.

I am also confused
About a few things,
Like why my spouse claims
That I have mood swings.

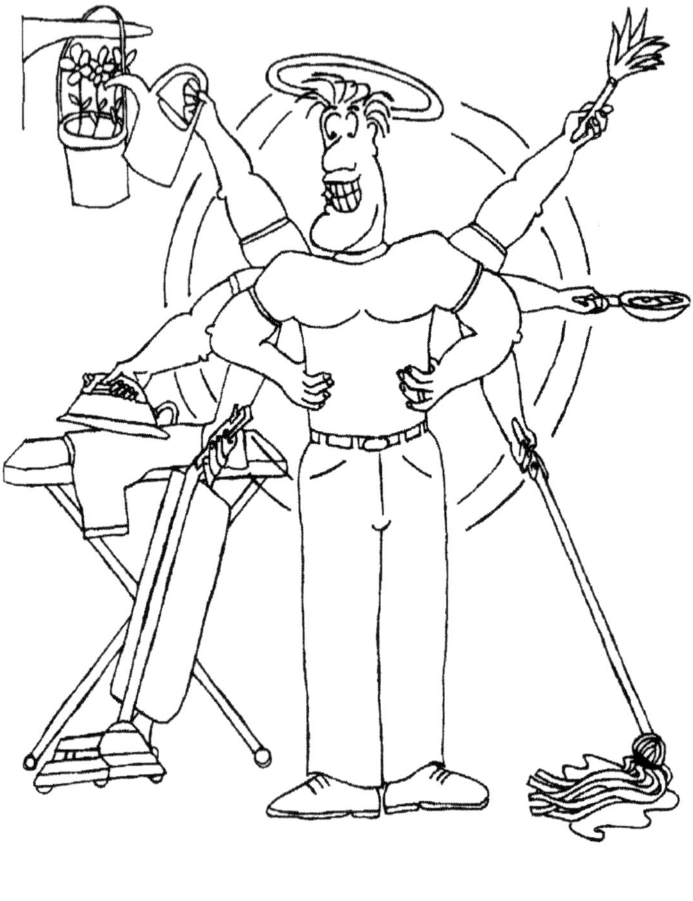

St. Hubby

"Hello, Honey
I've had a rough day,
Could I have a massage
And, oh, by the way,

While you're in the kitchen,
Could you cook me some food,
And don't take too long
I don't mean to sound rude.

Could you grab a blanket,
And also a chair,
To prop up my feet
I hope this is fair,

To ask of you dear
Yet another request,
The food you have cooked
Needs a little more zest.

Zip off to the store
I need you to go,
But don't leave just yet
I want you to know,

Remember the mail
We received yesterday,
Many bills came
That you need to pay.

And could you please tackle
That big laundry pile,
It seems it's been sitting
On our floor for awhile.

Then on your way down
To our laundry room,
Could you grab a mop
And of course a vacuum.

Our house really needs
A dust and a sweep,
Be careful because
Our stairs are quite steep.

I'm sorry, Honey...
Was there something you said...
Goodnight, my beloved...
I must go to bed."

Mr. Scale is a Liar

I'm certain my friend
Mr. Scale likes to lie,
It seems that my weight
Is a little bit high.

I'm certain he's added
A pound here and there,
He smiles at my face
When I look down in despair.

I'm sure when he
Tells me my weight,
That he is a liar
Who doesn't talk straight.

After I step
On the scale for a reading,
I know that he laughs
Until late in the evening.

It's really quite sad
That he acts in this manner,
He's lucky I haven't
Let him meet Mr. Hammer.

And I will take pity
On this poor little guy,
Yet to replace him
The price is not high.

So listen up, Mr. Scale,
When you tell me my weight,
You better be honest
Or you'll meet a dark fate.

Carrying Low or Carrying Behind

"Doctor, oh Doctor,
Could I please have a word,
This is going to sound odd
And even absurd.

I have an inquiry
That needs your attention,
Quite frankly it's something
I'd rather not mention.

This question is not easy
For me now to raise,
It's something I noticed
Over the past few days.

You may have detected
My rear is quite large,
To be rather honest
It resembles a barge.

Has it ever been noted
Or medically documented,
This is going to seem strange
And even demented.

But I have a feeling
That I'm turned around,
I believe that a baby
In my bottom abounds.

Yes, what I am saying
I swear to be true,
And I'm seeking some science
And proof, please, from you.

Is it possible my baby
Now grows in my rear,
It appears all my weight
Is travelling there.

I know, my dear Doctor,
You think I'm a nut,
But I'm certain a baby
Resides in my butt.

Cricket

My legs are changing
They're getting quite thick,
Their circumference swells larger
With every clock tick.

I merely look at food
And they start to grow,
My legs they do reap
What food I do sow.

I've heard it's reserve
For when baby arrives,
The food I have stored
Will help him survive.

My limbs seem like trunks
And are dense like a thicket,
My legs rub together
Like a spastic cricket.

Yes, my friends
My legs hum and sing,
When my thighs rub together
They make a sharp ring.

Ms. Wonder Bra...
See Ya', Wouldn't
Want to Be Ya'

All right this is something
That's brand new to me,
A bra size of "A"
Has morphed to a "C."

Never knew cleavage
Look at this chest,
Of everything in pregnancy
This is the best.

Now my friend, Ms. Wonder Bra,
Could I have a word with you,
At this time a separation
Is certainly due.

I'm off on my own
Don't need you to wear,
Suddenly, I've been blessed
With quite a nice pair.

I don't mean to sound flippant
Someday you'll be back,
But presently I'm enjoying
My bodacious new rack.

Stretch to the Moon

A pull here
Yet another pull there,
My body is stretching
To be blunt, everywhere.

It seems that baby
Is just making room,
So he can soon coast
On out of my womb.

I tell you it smarts
It hurts a great deal,
My ligaments are stretching
With unbounded zeal.

Some tell me that this
Is just nature's way,
And I will continue
To stretch every day.

I assure you that this
Is not doom and gloom,
But my hips have spread
They're as wide as the moon.

Although this stretching
May be right on track,
One question remains
Will my body stretch back?

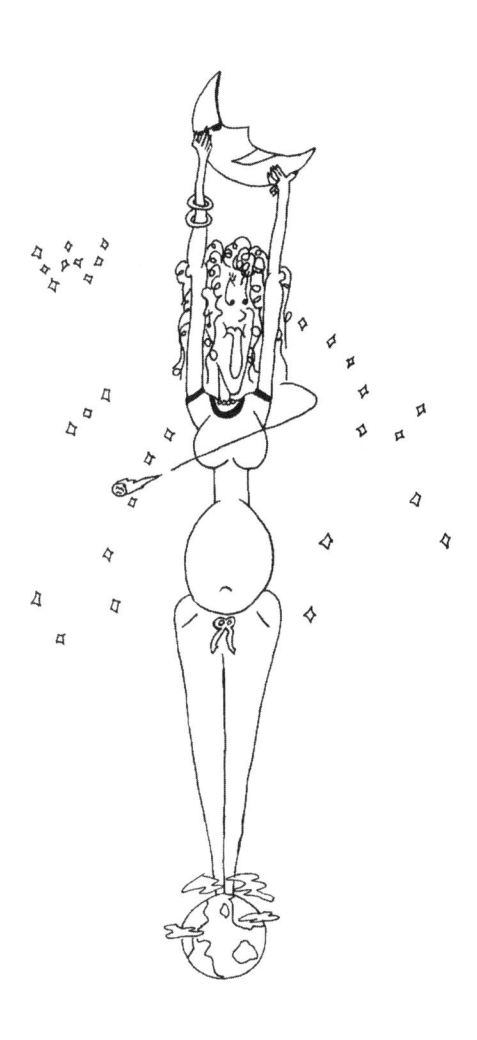

Incredible Shrinking Bladder

My bladder has shrunken
To a very small state,
Every hour I squat
And then eliminate.

Sixty minutes pass
And again I retreat,
To perch right on top
Of my toilet seat.

If I drink a little
It matters not,
Within but an hour,
I'll be on the pot.

I realize I'm ridding
My body of waste,
And off to the bathroom
I run with much haste.

Yet the other day,
A problem arose,
I discovered the existence
Of a leak in my hose.

You see something happened
By unfortunate chance,
A flood of liquid
Ran right through my pants.

It was rather sudden
My nose did a sneeze,
My urine flooded out
And did so with ease.

It flowed down my leg
And onto the floor,
And then it splashed up
All over the door.

I stood in the doorway
Feeling quite sick,
And thought it sure stinks
That I am a chick.

So This Is Heartburn

Oh my goodness...
My throat it does burn,
It seems my stomach
Has taken a turn.

What is this feeling
Deep within my throat,
Lining my airways
Is a fiery coat.

It's like I'm downing
An acidic slurp,
Here it comes
Oh NO...BURRRRP!

Probably shouldn't have
All those spicy meals,
If this is how
They can make me feel.

I never thought that
My throat could ever churn,
I'm not even 30
And I've got heartburn.

Back Attack

Oh the aches
And pains in my back,
The bulge in my belly
Has me out of whack.

A torment exists
In my back's lower part,
The cramp hasn't stopped
Since the day it did start.

Beginning up high and
Then moving down low,
The pain doth persist
With a constant flow.

Sometimes this agony
It seems everywhere,
And never, no never,
Does it disappear.

I wish that I
Could get some help,
Cuz' whenever I stand
You'll hear me yelp.

Now don't you worry
And don't you dare frown,
It's simply not as bad
As it surely sounds.

When I complain
It feels so good,
If you hurt like this,
I bet you would.

Zebra's Pride

In the fields of Africa,
The zebra does graze,
His black and white colors
Are sure to amaze.

You'll notice many people
Will give lots of hype,
To his vertical lines
Existing as stripes.

I would concur
They're a wonder to see,
But stripes on my body
Look not nice on me.

Yes, I now have stripes
Though not black and white,
They exist on my stomach
From left side to right.

They delicately lie
Across both my thighs,
They vary in number
And differ in size.

The zebra is proud
For his stripes help him hide,
But for me these darn stretchmarks
Are no source of pride.

Hail to the Hoover Dam

In the state of Nevada,
The Hoover Dam you can see,
But when it comes to water,
It retains less than me.

My feet and hands are swollen
They've ballooned everywhere,
Looking like this forever
Is my dreaded fear.

My face is very puffy
I now have countless chins,
When battling retention
The water always wins.

It settles in my cells
And deep within my thighs,
With every passing day,
My water levels rise.

And if the dam of Nevada,
Should ever run dry,
I've a guaranteed solution
And this is no lie.

Should our nation ever suffer
A drought emergency,
The country can find a reservoir
I've stored internally.

Ode to My In-Laws

Ode to my in-laws
They can be so kind,
I love when they comment
On the size of my behind.

It seems they are consumed
With my daily changing weight,
They say they are concerned
That I have a healthy state.

"You're looking pretty big
How much more weight did you gain,
We know all our comments
Do not cause you any pain.

Why, when we come over
Do you always seem so tense,
Now don't you be embarassed
Just because you are immense.

What did you say you're up to...
What's your new size,
Have you recently taken
A look at your thighs?

We talked to our son
As you know, he's your spouse,
But he has not observed
That you now dwarf a house.

But don't you worry, dear,
We are here for you right now,
We'll be certain to remind you
That you're bigger than a sow."

And don't you worry in-laws
A message straight from me,
If you keep calling me fat,
Your grandson you won't see.

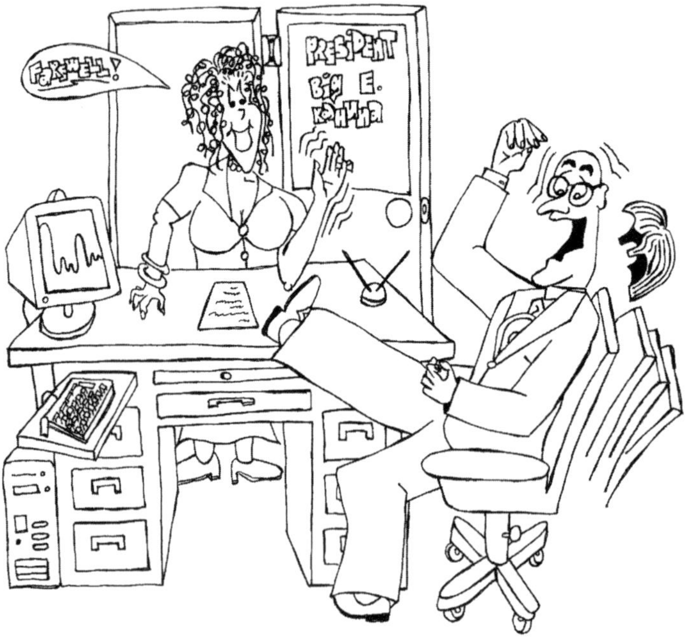
FAREWELL!
PRESIDENT
BIG E.
KAHUNA

Maternity Leave...
Also Known as
Short Term Disability

My dear sweet boss
Do you think I could deceive,
And not return to work
After taking eight week leave?

How much I'd miss the boys' club
Exclusively for men,
And how they degrade women
Over and over again.

I'd truly miss each and every
Misogynous attack,
And how they take a knife
And plunge it in one's back.

There's quite a lot of love
They're full of group hugs,
It's clear when they discuss
The size of our jugs.

And as you are aware,
You're full of sensitivity,
Especially when discussing
Matters of maternity.

You laugh at women's pains
From labor's infancy,
A shame you can't go through
Nine months of pregnancy.

But I have revenge planned
This book is going to sell,
And soon I'll walk into the office
And say "NOW GO TO...farewell."

Just Looking

Off to the baby store
I swiftly did run,
I thought to myself
It sure might be fun.

I'll just skip on over
And see what is there,
Check out some more cribs
And maybe high chairs.

I won't buy a thing
I'll just take a gaze,
When I walked in the store,
I was most amazed.

I started to look
Extended my arm,
One toy in the cart
Won't do any harm.

That outfit is cute
And that one is, too,
I won't shop so long
I've got much to do.

I'll just browse for awhile
Won't buy any stuff,
To look without buying
Is really quite rough.

Oooo, that would look nice
On the nursery wall,
Of course another object
In the cart takes a fall.

I sure am fatigued
In my bed I must crash,
I never thought looking
Would cost so much cash.

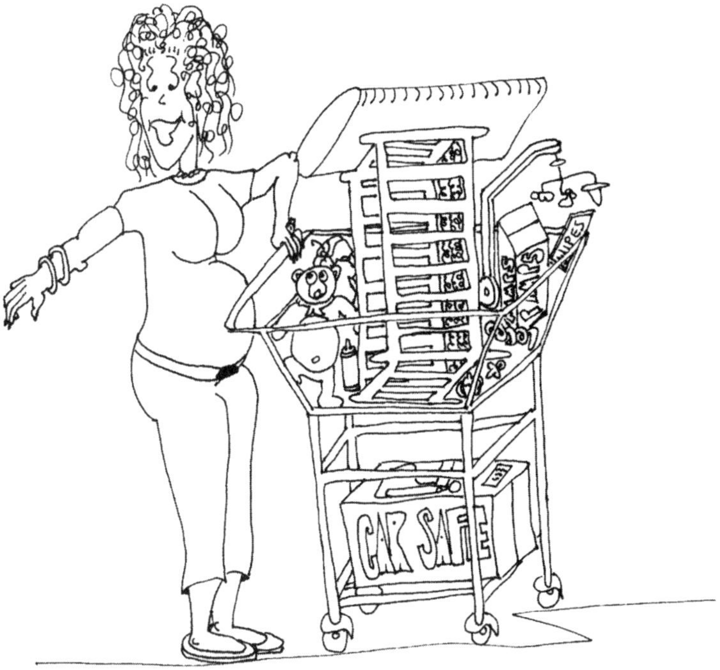
CAR SAFE

Birthing Class

The couples walk in
Two by two,
You can see in their faces
They're not sure what to do.

A new topic emerges
In every class,
This is a test
They know they must pass.

"Are you having a girl
We are having a boy,
Have you heard about the latest
And greatest new toy?"

Breastfeeding, diapers,
And of course newborn care,
The delivery topic
Is more than some can bear.

They listen intensely
Every word from the proctor,
Anxious to question
Their very own doctor.

At the end of class,
They breathe to relax,
Praying their minds
Will retain all the facts.

One day soon,
Their labor will be live,
And they just hope
That they can survive.

Who Wants To Be a Milkingaire?

The lactation counselor
Walks into the room,
"BREAST IS BEST,"
Her voice loudly booms.

"Breast milk is better
Than formula as food,
Of this I am certain
I would never delude.

I don't care if it hurts
It's worth all the pain,
If you do not breastfeed,
Then you are insane.

And should an infection
Occur in one breast,
Switch to the other cuz'
BREAST IS STILL BEST.

If you work full-time
There's no need to fear,
Breast pumps are available
For one or a pair.

I will counsel you
And give loads of advice,
Of my information
Please don't you think twice.

Nursing mothers rule
Naturally...the best,
I challenge you,
Put your breast to the test.

Way to go, gal,
To you, my sweet dear,
Congratulations are in order
For the new "Milkingaire!"

Shower Power

To the right are some cookies
To the left fruit tea,
Today this shower
Will focus on me.

We'll play some games
And guess baby's weight,
Many are guessing
The baby's due date.

Relatives all ask
"How are you feeling dear,
Labor really hurts
Though there's nothing to fear."

I open each gift
Another onesie I receive,
Loads of presents
Cuz' I did conceive.

I try to behave
And act so polite,
It's only midday
But feels like midnight.

Lots of talking
Loads of advice,
To do this again
I'd have to think twice.

The flowers are pretty
The food has been great,
Yet for another shower
I think I can wait.

Hands Off

My unborn child
Isn't public domain,
From your touch
I prefer to refrain.

Strangers all say
"You're pregnant I see,"
And then they move in
So they can touch me.

"Excuse me, pal,
Move your hand from my belly,"
This should be a crime
And probably a felony!

How would you feel
Were I to touch you,
Without your permission
Now what would you do?

Now that I'm pregnant
It seems you believe,
That my womb is waiting
For your hand to receive.

The truth of it is
My body is mine,
And without your fondling,
I'll get along fine.

Mystery Of The Mucus Plug

One day in the toilet,
It appears like lightning,
It's a strange spectacle
And most certainly frightening.

It's bloody and ugly
And in a big chunk,
The sight of it simply
Spirals you into a funk.

From research you learn
It's not crazy or wild,
Yes, this is just normal
When you are with child.

The mucus plug
Is officially its name,
And over the years
It's acquired some fame.

You see its appearance
Just may be a sign,
That your body's ready
And maybe it's time.

The mucus plug it once
Was a mere mystery,
Is now on its way to make
Toilet bowl history.

(((FLUSH!!!)))

Tis The Night Before Due Date

'Tis the night before due date
And all through the house,
The only one sleeping
Is my faithful spouse.

I just cannot slumber
As in months before,
At three in the morning,
I'm doing house chores.

No wonder I can't sleep
My hormones are raging,
Every minute of the day
My body is changing.

I awake this night
And think, "What should I do,"
It's surely too early
To let coffee brew.

So I open a book
About labor I read,
There are many warnings
To which I must heed.

Of course all this reading
Gets me in a fit,
I no longer have
The patience to sit.

I walk around the house
Inspect every room,
Awaiting some action
From my body's womb.

And soon I see
The rise of the sun,
My due date has now
Officially begun.

I sit and gaze
At the clock all day,
Waiting for a baby
What's with the delay?

Soon the sun falls
The sky turns to black,
And three in the morning
Does quickly come back.

Post-Due Date Blues

Will it be today
Or maybe tonight,
I'm hoping soon
To have you in my sight.

They say I'm effaced
And truly so well dilated,
Yet day after day
I'm fetally constipated.

A contraction here
A contraction there,
Some bloody show
On my underwear.

Another hour does pass
Time runs so slow,
When will you come
I just need to know.

You're probably aware
You must know the news,
I've got what they call
The post due date blues.

Fetus Philosophy 101

I think my baby
Worries for his fate,
I think that's why
He's past his due date.

He hears the world
The good and the bad,
He hears the joyful
But also the sad.

He sits in my womb
And wonders all day,
"Is this a place
Where I want to stay?"

He knows of the gluttony
And all of the greed,
And on top of that,
There's pressure to succeed.

Then he hears music
A beautiful song,
And thinks there's a chance
That he can belong,

To a world of wonder
And sweet melody,
Yes, he is now thinking
That he is ready.

He then sees the good
And watches it prevail,
He's certain that evil
Can't help but fail.

So he now decides
That soon he'll arrive,
Certain he knows
That with love he'll survive.

Rated PreGnant

A movie star I'm not
Now this you'll perceive,
I do not want a strange
VHS tape of me.

When I am in labor
I'll be in great pain,
From a video of labor
I'd rather abstain.

It would be full of blood,
Gunk, and some pus,
This is a matter
I will not discuss.

Don't get me wrong
Birthing is beauty,
But to get it on tape
Is just not my duty.

So put away your camera
The action, and lights,
A film of my privates
Won't be shot that night.

Vroom...

If the light is red
I do not care,
Your job St. Hubby,
Is to get me there.

Forget the stop signs
And all of the lights,
Ignore the speed limit
Those signs are a blight.

Every contraction is rough
Can you hear my plea,
I need an epidural
Inserted in me.

So push the petal
On down to the floor,
Get me quickly
To the hospital door.

No, I'm not yelling
So kindly shut up,
I think that my body's
About to erupt.

Hoo Hoo Hoo...
Hee Hee Hee,
Breathing exercises
Don't seem to work for me.

Finally, we're here
A nurse sees I'm hellish,
She's putting on gloves
To look at my pelvis.

She looks up and smirks
Her words cut like a saber,
"You've not even begun
The start of your labor."

Womb with a View

To wash your hands
There is a sink,
In the corner sits
A couch that is pink.

It folds on out
And into a bed,
So hubby can rest
His poor weary head.

A monitor with lines
Is right here on my side,
My bed extends
Surprise, it's extra wide.

A baby scale has
A warming lamp,
To dry my baby
When he's still damp.

The room is sterile
It's extra clean,
They've hooked me to
Another machine.

A VCR,
A new T.V.,
This room comes with
A hefty fee.

The rate is high
It's much to pay,
But I believe
That it's worth the stay.

For I would offer
A million and one,
To birth in comfort
My new baby son.

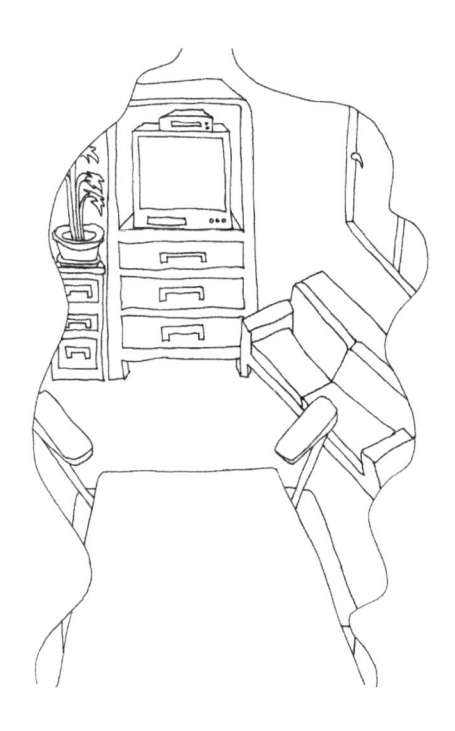

Assault On My Uterus

Every contraction grows
Ever more intense,
I'm thinking this child
Just must be immense.

I try to be stoic
And take all the pain,
"I don't need an epidural,"
I calmly explain.

This is a breeze
No, this is not bad,
Why are you looking
At me like I'm mad?

Whoa...wait a second,
I'm changing my mind,
An anesthetist is needed
You quickly must find,

That man with the needle
To put in my back,
I believe that my uterus
Is under attack.

These breathing exercises
Still don't seem to work,
I glare at my husband
And call him a jerk.

You did this to me
Look at me now,
He stares at me strangely
And raises his brow.

His wife has turned into
A whole different creature,
She's lacking right now
One redeemable feature.

Finally, salvation
Arrives at my side,
Slowly in my back
A syringe does glide.

Ah this is nice
I'm feeling quite numb,
I no longer believe
My husband's a bum.

In fact he is kind,
Caring and sweet,
He's helping me accomplish
A wonderful feat.

What was that...
Wait, a feeling below,
Something is moving
And it's moving quite low.

The nurse comes in
It's time for a check,
She sits down and turns
Her head and her neck.

She takes a glance
Her eyes open wide,
"It's time to push,"
And she'll be my guide.

In come five people
And the doctor, too,
Everyone's telling me
What I should do.

"PUSH-PUSH-PUSH
You can't give up yet,"
My body is boiling
And covered with sweat.

Someone yells loudly
Out into the air,
"Here he comes
He's got loads of hair!"

I push real hard
With all of my heart,
And then out he comes
I feel every part.

He wiggles on out
I hear not a cry,
I'm suddenly asking
The question of "Why?"

Why don't I hear him
Someone tell me why,
But the air is soon pierced
By a most welcome cry.

The most beautiful cry
How it soothes my soul,
And on down my cheeks
The tears start to roll.

They hand him to me
A small fragile being,
I hardly believe
The angel I'm seeing.

I can't even explain
The love that I feel,
I've already forgotten
This painful ordeal.

Now I am focused
On a wonderful boy,
This is the precious
True meaning of joy.

I look at him calmly
And think life's begun,
Yes, anything is possible
For you, my dear son.

Not Sew Good

Knit one
Pearl two,
Sewing me up
Is what Doc has to do.

Doc thinks my body
Is for him to sew,
He stitches up high
Before proceeding down low.

This is quite lovely
I can feel every stitch,
To a thinner needle
Could we possibly switch?

Yes, I'm embarrassed
And feeling quite weird,
If he poked at your privates
I know you'd be scared.

But not to worry
Soon he'll be done,
And I can get on
To admiring my son.

Oooo...Ouch
Some more tugs to go,
"Things look good,"
Doc yells from below.

Sure they look good
Easy for him to say,
Could you just finish
And then be on your way?

I've never been fond
Of a needle, you see,
And haven't enjoyed having
This natal embroidery.

Gotta Run

A baby I've got
So I've gotta scoot,
From start to finish
This sure's been a hoot!

From Something's Amiss
To A Test You Can't Study,
To Me, a Couch, Will It,
And a Porcelain buddy.

To Pyramids and
Extra Extra Read All About It,
We heard a Whoosh
There ain't no doubt about it.

To Lights, Camera, Adorable
And What's in a Name,
To Kicks and to Moodswings
That make you insane.

To St. Hubby and of course
To a Scale that does Lie,
To Carrying Behind
Instead of too high.

To a Cricket, a new Bra
And a Stretch To the Moon,
And a Shrinking Bladder
That goes often too soon.

To Heartburn, a bad Back
And new Zebra Stripes,
To the Hoover Dam and In-Laws
And all of their hype.

To Maternity Leave, and
Just taking a Look,
To a Milkingaire
And the Birthing Class book.

To Showers and Hands Off
And the Mucus Plug,
To the Night Before Due Date
And the Post-Due Date bug.

To Fetus Philosophy
And Rated P.G.,
To Vroom and a Womb
With a View you should see.

To Assault on My Uterus
And a doctor to Sew,
To writing this book
While I'm on the go.

Hope you've enjoyed this
But I've gotta run,
You hear all that crying...
Yep, that's my new son!

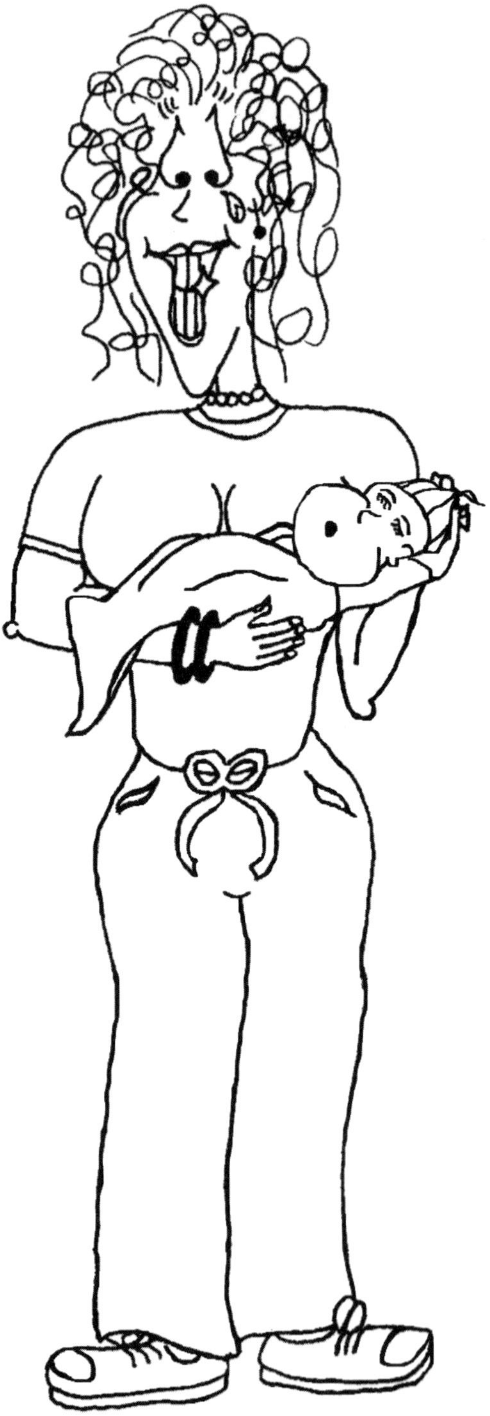

INDEX

Assault On My Uterus, 93-97

Back Attack, 52-53
Birthing Class, 67-68

Carrying Low or Carrying Behind, 38-40
Cricket, 41-42

**Extra, Extra Read All About It.
    Everyone's Got An Opinion And I
    Don't Want It**, 19-21

Fetus Philosophy 101, 84-86

Gotta Run, 100-102

Hail to the Hoover Dam, 56-57
Hands Off, 75-76

Incredible Shrinking Bladder, 47-49

Just Looking, 64-66

Kick Away, 29-30

Lights_Camera_Adorable, 27-28

Maternity Leave Also Known as
 Short Term Disability, 61-63
ME, 6-8
Mood Swings, 31-32
Mr. Couch is No Slouch, 9-10
Mr. Scale is a Liar, 36-37
Ms. Wonder Bra See Ya Would'nt Want
 To Be Ya, 43-44
Mystery Of The Mucus Plug, 77-78

Not Sew Good, 98-99

Ode to My In-Laws, 58-60

Porcelain Party, 17-18
Post-Due Date Blues, 82-83
Pregnancy Food Pyramid, 14-16

Rated PreGnant, 87-88

Shower Power, 72-74
So This Is Heartburn, 50-51
Something's Amiss in My Uterus, 1-2
St. Hubby, 33-35
Stretch to the Moon, 45-46

The Test for Which You Can't
 Study, 3-5
'Tis The Night Before Due Date, 79-81

Vroom, 89-90

What's in a Name?, 24-26
Who Wants To Be A Milkingaire, 69-71
Whoosh, 22-23
Will It...? 11-13
Womb With a View, 91-92

Zebra's Pride, 54-55

Acknowledgements

I would like to thank my husband for coming into my life and staying there. Believe me when I tell you it is the most difficult task in the world. I thank him for his wonderful illustrations...without his talent this book would be seriously lacking. I would also like to thank my siblings, Jody, Missy, Ben, Josh, and Seth for their tireless edits and selling efforts. I would like to thank my mother for her amazing sense of humor, and my father for his incredible work ethic. These two traits are the driving force behind this book. Yes, I know I make fun of my in-laws in this book, but I tell ya, I am darn lucky! I thank them for pushing me to take this book to the next level and for believing in me, when I doubted myself. Many thanks to Bradley Kale who worked diligently on this book, without his help I would have been lost. Finally, I thank Clint Greenleaf in advance for helping me to distribute this book to the millions of people who I know will be lined up to buy it.

About the Author

Photo: Rusty Rust, Nashville, TN

Written with rhythmic candor, "Something's Amiss in My Uterus" lightens any pregnant woman's plight by taking her on an authentic journey through the trying times of pregnancy. This humorous compilation of poems began while Hodes was struggling as a rookie financial advisor during the worst bear market in stock market history. Aching to escape corporate America so she could reconnect with her newborn son, Hodes wrote the book with a pen and a prayer. She turned to her husband, renowned glassblower Scott Hodes, to put her ideas into illustrations. The couple's synergy has resulted in a whimsical book of poetry that brings smiles, tears, and laughter to every reader.

Pregnancy Notes:

Date:	Event:	I can relate to this poem:

Pregnancy Notes:

Date:	Event:	I can relate to this poem:

Ordering Information

To order <u>Something's</u> <u>Amiss</u> <u>In</u> <u>My</u> <u>Uterus</u>, email your name, address, and phone number to someamiss@aol.com or complete order form below.

- -

Payable in U.S. funds only. Book price: $12.00. Postage and handling is $3.00 per book. Mail check or money order payable to Hilary Hodes and send to:

Hilary Hodes
P.O. Box 92
Fairview, TN 37062

Name:_____

Address:_____

City:_____State:_____Zip:_____

Phone:_____

Quantity: _____

Book Total: $_____

Postage and Handling: $_____

Applicable Sales Tax $_____

Total Amount Due: $_____

- -

Thank you for your order!